Our Duty and Our Joy

The Sacrifice of Praise

ROBERT LLEWELYN

... it is our duty and our joy, at all times and in all places,
to give you thanks and praise ...

Alternative Service Book

Let us continually offer to God a sacrifice of praise.

Hebrews 13:15

Save and help us that we may praise you.

Alternative Service Book

DARTON · LONGMAN + TODD

First published in 1993 by
Darton, Longman and Todd Ltd
1 Spencer Court
140–142 Wandsworth High Street
London SW18 4JJ

Reprinted 1995

ISBN 0–232–52050–X

A catalogue record for this book is
available from the British Library

Thanks are due to the following for permission to quote copyright
material: Hodder & Stoughton, from *Prison to Praise* by Merlin
Carothers; Kingsway from *Power in Praise* by Merlin Carothers
(1974). Quotations from the *Revelations of Divine Love* are adapted
by the author from *Julian of Norwich: Revelations of Divine Love* by
Clifton Wolters, Penguin (1966), and *All Shall Be Well* by Shelia
Upjohn, Darton, Longman and Todd (1992).

The author is grateful to Mr Adrian Morgan for permission to use
his beautiful photograph of 'The Glory', which forms the central
part of the reredos at St Michael's Church, Framlingham; also to
Revd Richard Willcock, Rector of St Michael's, for his permission
to use the painting.

Phototypeset in $9^1/_2$/11pt Palatino by Intype, London
Printed and bound in Great Britain
by Page Bros, Norwich

Contents

Preface

I recall how a priest to whom I appealed during a particularly testing time advised me to try thanking God for everything. 'And I mean *everything*', he added, giving emphasis to the final word.[1] I started off with good intentions but soon discovered that in congenial circumstances they were easily forgotten, whereas in those which were fearful or painful I often lacked the faith or courage.

But that the advice was good I have never doubted and I believe it to be a key element in Christian living. It may not be the only stone which 'turneth all to gold',[2] but certainly it is one, and many would consider it to be the most precious one of all. In Isaiah's vision of the city of the Lord the walls were named Salvation: its entrance was called Praise. (Isaiah 60:14, 18)

Some may think that in the pages which follow I have stretched the bow too far. But however it may be in practice, for few are seasoned archers, it seems to me it must be capable of being stretched the whole way or not at all. Otherwise, instead of being free to turn to praise at once, we would constantly be left wondering on which side of the divide we stood as the events of life unfolded.

Whereas Paul, on whose bidding this book is based, was called to experience the mountain peaks, it is likely that most readers will, with the author, find the daily training on the nursery slopes tests their stamina to its limits. It is for such people that this book is offered. Our prayer will be that God, knowing our frailty, will mercifully protect us from trials beyond our capacity to bear.

It is a stupendous task to which Paul calls the Church: to thank and praise God for everything. Sometimes, no doubt, even for Paul, that could only be done in retrospect. In the eleventh chapter of his second epistle to the Corinthians Paul recalls events which would test the hardiest to the limits of endurance. Doubtless, together we shall want to cry: 'Lord, if thy presence go not with me, carry us not up hence.' (Exodus 33:15)

Prologue from William Law

The Perfection of all virtues

As thankfulness is an express acknowledgement of the goodness of God towards you, so repinings and complaints are as plain accusations of God's want and goodness toward you.

Would you know who is the greatest saint in the world? It is not he who prays most or fasts most, it is not he who gives most alms or is most eminent for temperance, chastity or justice; but it is he who is always thankful to God, who wills everything that God wills, who receives everything as an instance of God's goodness and has a heart always ready to praise God for it.

All prayer and devotion, fastings and repentance, meditation and retirement, all sacraments and ordinances are but so many means to render the soul . . . conformable to the will of God and to fill it with thankfulness and praise for everything that comes from God. This is the perfection of all virtues, and all virtues that do not tend to it or proceed from it are but so many false ornaments of a soul not converted to God.

If anyone would tell you the shortest, surest way to all happiness and all perfection, he must tell you to make it a rule to yourself to thank and praise God for everything that happens to you. For it is certain that whatever seeming calamity happens to you, if you thank and praise God for it, you turn it into a blessing. Could you therefore work miracles, you could not do more for yourself than by this thankful spirit, for it . . . turns all that it touches into happiness.[3]

Praise and thanksgiving

Meister Eckhart, who is much in vogue today, has given praise and thanksgiving, whatever the circumstances, as the first of five hallmarks which characterise a truly Christian life.

A more recent writer on the New Testament, John Koenig, describes praise and thanksgiving as its heart-beat, 'a pulsating centre that pumps life into the whole body'.[4]

In the power of praise and thanksgiving the early Church was carried forward, uplifted and sustained. It was as it should be in every age.

You may note that praise and thanksgiving have been linked three times. It is useful to have the two words though it is difficult to distinguish between them.

Praise and thanksgiving, like faith and hope, peace and joy, flow into one another at every point. You cannot have an abundance of one without a deep experience of the other.

Praise and thanksgiving stand or fall together. In thanking God, the heart is moved to praise; in praising him, thanksgiving overflows.

In the pages which follow, where one word is used the other is implied. If a distinction were possible, we might say that we praise God in a situation for what he is, and we thank him for what he is doing to bring the matter to its best conclusion.

Giving thanks in everything

Writing to the Thessalonians (1 Thessalonians 5:18), Paul bids his readers to give thanks *in* everything. To the Ephesians (Ephesians 5:20), he says they are to give thanks *for* all things. There is a distinction between the two, though perhaps that is seldom recognised. Let me try to explain.

Suppose John (as we may call him) were put into prison for a crime which he did not commit. Someone has made up false and malicious stories against him and has persuaded the court that they were true.

If John is accustomed to praising God in everything, it makes little sense that he should now cease simply because he is on the other side of the prison walls. He will continue to praise God in these circumstances, whether outwardly in attending services in the prison chapel, or inwardly in the silent uplifting of the heart.

There is no problem here, that is to say there is no theological problem, though other problems springing from the challenge and distress of the situation may, of course, arise.

But at least John knows what he ought to do, however far he may fall short in its performance.

Giving thanks for everything

But can John give thanks *for* the circumstances of prison? It was, after all, the malice and lies of another which put him there.

Since evil can never be praiseworthy John will perhaps conclude that whilst he can praise God *in* the circumstances of prison he is unable to praise God *for* them. On theological grounds the praising of God for his imprisonment would be ruled out.

But if John came to such a conclusion he would be wrong. Evil, it is true, is not praiseworthy, but that God should allow evil, that is praiseworthy. God has endowed us with free will, and in allowing us to abuse it, even to the committing of horrendous crimes, he is honouring his gift.[5]

We may conclude, therefore, that John is, theologically speaking, on firm ground in thanking God *for* his imprisonment, and not simply in giving thanks *in* the circumstances of captivity.

This is not nit-picking. It is important that the truth should be established. It sets praise free from any limitations which might be placed upon it, and it sets the one who praises free from introspective enquiry as to whether what he is doing is justifiable or not. The chances are we would never offer praise in uncongenial circumstances if we needed first to enquire whether praise was permissible.

Of course we must be clear to ourselves that in every case we are praising *God* in and for the circumstances. We are not praising the circumstances themselves, which may, or may not, be praiseworthy.

Paul and Silas in prison

We return to Paul. We are to give thanks to God in everything and for everything. These instructions are given in isolated texts, but they are in keeping with the spirit of Paul's writing. And not only in keeping with his writing but, as we would expect, with his life.

We may recall how Paul and Silas suffered imprisonment at Philippi (Acts 16:25–34). At midnight, held in the stocks, smarting from the wounds of their flogging, they sing out their praises to God. In the Philippian jail we see the two Pauline texts we have quoted lifted from the papyrus and translated into life.

Often when we praise God in and for an adverse situation it is totally unclear how any good may flow from it. We offer praise in the power of faith, thus placing the situation in God's hands and laying ourselves open in the fullest manner possible to respond to the outpouring of his grace. Doubtless it was so with Paul and Silas that night in the Philippian jail. In their case the fruits of praise were not long delayed. Before the day was out the jailer was converted and he and his household were baptised.

Sometimes, however, it may be years, or even never on this side of death, before we see our faith vindicated.

The triumph is in the praise

I owe to Father Benson ssje, founder of the community popularly known as the Cowley Fathers, a saying which has for some years greatly influenced my life: 'We do not praise God because he has caused us to triumph, but because to praise God *is* to triumph.'[6]

Looking back to the illustration given, there was no triumph, as the world sees it, in Paul and Silas finding themselves in prison. The triumph was not in the situation but in praising God in and for the situation.

Moving from the spiritual heights to circumstances with which we are familiar, if I find myself in the supermarket queue in which the three people in front of me insist on paying by cheque, that is hardly a triumph when I might have chosen my queue more wisely.

But to praise God in that situation *is* to triumph.

After all, I have often prayed for patience, and here is God answering my prayer by giving me an opportunity in which to exercise it.

The creative function of praise

The test proposed may not be particularly challenging. Arriving at the station just as the train is departing may place a greater strain on my resources. Yet here again is an opportunity for patience, and God may have other purposes in the enforced delay.

Perhaps I shall meet someone on the next train whom I would otherwise have missed, and perhaps this meeting will be of great significance to me or the other.

But in all honesty we have to say that it is more likely that we shall never discover any secondary purpose for our delay. The lesson may be no other than that we should get our act together in the matter of catching trains.

However, it remains true that the one who praises God in all circumstances is truly blessed; and not least by being best prepared for meeting constructively events which may flow from them.

Of course there has to be a desire for marriage between heart and lips – and marriages have to be worked at, and may take a lifetime in coming to completion.

You must be joking

But, you may be thinking, surely you can't be serious? Do you really mean I'm to praise God when held up in the queue? Even more, when I miss my train? I suppose I could make the movements with my lips, but I'd feel so superficial, so unreal.

Yes, I am entirely serious and I know just how you feel. What you have mentioned is the persistent temptation in the matter of praising God in all circumstances. It is well to see from the start what a cheat this temptation is.

Think a moment! If you and I feel unreal when we start praising, that doesn't mean we have suddenly become unreal. It means we were unreal before, and the praising has made us realise it.

It makes no sense to say that five seconds before praising you were a real person and five seconds after you were unreal. God doesn't change us as rapidly as that!

So what praising has done is to help us to realise our unreality. And that little bit of self-knowledge is valuable for it shows us how much we need to move towards what is real.

That is what life is about: the movement towards the real. All praise, so long as it is well-intentioned – no matter about the feelings – assists that movement.

You are well-intentioned if you do but desire that your heart shall move in correspondence with your lips or thoughts. Or even if you can but desire to desire that this shall be so.

Praise goes beyond submission or acceptance

The well-known spiritual director Jean-Pierre de Caussade would advise the sisters in his care to praise God for the sufferings and ordeals they were called upon to bear. If, however, they found this to be beyond them he would urge them to submit with such good grace as they were able.

In submission to our trials we reflect that everything ultimately flows from God, and that since he can will towards us only that which is good, it must follow that a blessing of which we may not now be aware will emerge from them if we can but accept them and co-operate with God in them.

Thus Caussade would offer the sisters a prayer such as: 'Lord, I accept as the blessing of your great mercy all pains which make my self-love suffer and all humiliations which crucify my pride.' To be able to use such a prayer genuinely is a great grace.

Praise, however, where it is true, is more positive than simple acceptance. Praise includes acceptance but goes beyond it. Praise releases power when the eye is on the giver and not the gift.

Praise and, in their measure, submission or acceptance, are self-emptying, whereas discontentedness, murmuring and the like are self-filling and root the practitioner more firmly in the self which needs to die that Christ may eternally be born anew.

What we have called the heart-beat of the New Testament is praise rather than submission or acceptance, and it is this to which its writers primarily call us.

The over-ruling Providence of God

It is clear that I have assumed that nothing happens by chance but by the over-ruling Providence of God.

That seems to be the teaching of Jesus who tells us that the hairs of our head are numbered, and that birds cannot fall to the ground without the Father knowing.

It is implicit in the writings of St Paul who sees himself as separated from his mother's womb (Galatians 1:15–16) to become an apostle to the Gentiles.

It has been the traditional teaching of the Church through the centuries. 'In the decree of God's Providence there is no chance. All is according to plan; all is directed to good.'[7]

It is taught repeatedly in the lives of the saints, perhaps nowhere more explicitly than in the writings of Julian of Norwich:

> I saw in truth that God does all things no matter how small they may be. And I saw that nothing happens by chance but by the far-sighted wisdom of God. If it seems like chance or accident to us it is because we are blind and blinkered. For the things planned by God before the world began (which he rightly and gloriously and continually shapes to the best end as they come about) come upon us suddenly and take us unawares. And so in our blindness or short-sightedness we say that these things are accident or chance. But to our Lord God they are not so. Therefore I must needs grant that everything that is done is done well, for it is God that does all.[8]

God's perpetual dilemma

Immediately before the foregoing quotation Julian wrote: 'I thought, "What is sin?" ' In writing that 'everything that is done is done well', Julian, therefore, includes sin, not of course because sin (which is evil) is praiseworthy, but because God's allowing sin is praiseworthy.

God's perpetual dilemma is how (having given us free will) he can, in the name of love, bring himself to refrain from cheating when all the cards seem to be in the hands of the enemy.[9]

But Julian is sure that God will win in the end. She would have agreed with St Augustine that God allows evil only to the extent to which it can be turned into good.

In chapter 13 of Julian's *Revelations* we have a quaintly amusing picture ('I laughed aloud, and those around me laughed too') of the devil working frantically to bring souls to perdition only to find that God, like a master chess player (my image) has a superior strategy, allowing faithful souls to escape his grasp by virtue of Christ's passion.

The devil becomes a pathetic figure. Having put heart and soul into his endeavours, he sees 'everything that God allows him to do turning to joy in us, but to shame and woe in him'.

It certainly cuts him down to size!

Praise the Lord, brother

Let me now return to our main theme. I recall how in my early twenties I stayed at a missionary training college in West Norwood. Everything was basic including its theology which was fundamentalist in the extreme. They asked me if I was a BA and expressed pleasure at my reply. It was only later that I discovered that the letters stood for 'born again'. Certainly these young men were truly renewed in Christ and I knew I had much to learn from them.

There was no regular income nor endowment. God was invoked to provide according to need. Fast days and feast days depended not on the calendar but on what arrived in the morning post. One day when the post failed to provide, a baker sent in twenty loaves saying he had miscalculated his requirements that morning.

I became friendly with George who, having a mission to perform in Scotland, asked me to drive him to Aberdeen. My father lent me his baby Austin car, and we set out together making the journey in several stages. George was a fairly silent passenger, but every few miles he would turn to me and say: 'Praise the Lord, brother. Keep praising.' Scotland was a long way off in those days, and perhaps I grew weary after a while. But there was no way of checking George's enthusiasm.

Start the engine, brother

The little car did us proudly until one evening after a broiling day the engine stalled on a lonely Highland hill. No effort of mine could get it started, and with dusk approaching I was getting anxious. Not so George. Taking his guitar he left the car, stood in front of the bonnet and sang a psalm to the Lord. His praises finished, he called to me to 'start the engine, brother', and to my surprise (though not, I suspect, to the reader's) it purred into life.

I am not suggesting a miracle but simply wanting to make the point that whilst the engine was cooling down, most of us would have been hotting up. But George had the secret. He never lost his composure and was as ready for the next stage as if nothing had happened.

Returning to Father Benson's great phrase, to stall the engine on a lonely Highland road was hardly to triumph, but to praise God in such circumstances was to triumph. And it would have remained a triumph even if the engine had failed to respond and we had been marooned for the night.

This last point is important for praise may never be seen as a way of manipulating God into giving us what we want. We praise God for the situation as it is, not for what we would like it to be. A pleasing outcome may be the consequence of praise but it is never to be its motivation.[10]

Praise in the power of faith

I trust another personal story will not be wearisome. It makes a further point which we must not miss.

I was, as an undergraduate, on the list at the University Appointments Board for work as a teacher. For reasons not relevant here I was particularly anxious to teach at a certain school at which a vacancy had arisen. I was interviewed with other candidates but not offered the post. I recall my dejection: no thought of thankfulness there!

A month later I was offered a post at another school and I knew at once that that was how it should be. The point, of course, is that unless we give thanks and praise to God in the power of faith and not of sight, whole periods of life will be lost.

The temptation is to forget that 'bad' weather has its blessing as well as that which is pleasing to the senses.

We thank and praise God easily enough when things go to our liking. Is there any test by which we may know that this praise is genuine, that it is truly for the glory of God, and is not simply an eruption of our unregenerate emotions?

Yes, there is a test and it is this. Are we also prompt in thanking and praising God when things go against the grain?

It is in returning thanks with such reality as is given us in areas within our reach that our hearts are enlarged to embrace situations now beyond us.

We are to pray for the gift of praise

The capacity to praise God in all seasons does not come naturally to us, but is a grace to be prayed for. George Herbert's poetic prayer has doubtless been a model for many:

> Thou that has given so much to me,
> Give one thing more, a grateful heart ...
> Not thankful when it pleases me,
> As though thy blessing had spare days;
> But such a heart whose pulse may be,
>   Thy praise.[11]

We may note that the poem is seeking the *spirit* of praise. Praise takes its value from the degree in which it is rooted in the heart. It is easy to praise God with words but they are valueless except in so far as they are used with the intention of engaging the heart in praise.

Alternatively, a powerful short prayer which might be on our lips at any time is: 'Save and help us that we may praise you',[12] Here we make explicit our desire for praise, at the same time acknowledging our insufficiency apart from God's grace. Following St Augustine who teaches that the desire for prayer is prayer, so the desire for praise is itself praise. We shall look at more direct forms of praise later.

We shall never get beyond the need of prayers such as these. For to praise God whatever happens is so earth-shaking a demand that probably only a saint (as was Paul) should command it, and certainly only a saint could fulfill it.

There are probably many who can look back to an event which looked shattering at the time but for which they are now truly grateful. But to praise God at the time! It may have been that not even Paul's courage and faith was equal to that in some situations.

Where do we begin?

It is, however, best to begin in areas of life where praise comes easily and naturally. This helps to form in us the habit of praise.

The following passage should open our awareness to the many opportunities of blessing through the day. It may be well to take several of the themes and weave them consciously into our praise of God.

> Lord of all Blessing,
> As we walk about your world,
> Let us know ourselves blessed at every turn;
> Blessed in the autumnal sun and leaves;
> Blessed in the winter wind;
> Blessed in rain and shafts of sunlight;
> Blessed in the moving stars;
> Blessed in the turning of the world
>   beneath our feet;
> Blessed in silence;
> Blessed in sleep;
> Blessed in our children, our parents and
>   our friends;
> Blessed in conversation and the human voice;
> Blessed in waiting for the bus, or train,
>   or traffic lights;
> Blessed in music, blessed in singing voices,
>   blessed in the song of birds;
> Blessed in the cry that pierces the heart;
> Blessed in the smile of strangers;
> Blessed in the touch of love, blessed in laughter;
> Blessed in pain, in darkness, in grief;
> Blessed in the desert and the frost;
> Blessed in waiting for the spring;
> Blessed in waiting and waiting and waiting.
> Lord of all blessing, we bless you.[13]

Julian and thanksgiving

Before we pass on, it is worth looking to see what Julian of Norwich has to say on praise and thanksgiving.[14]

In her brief treatment of thanksgiving (though her whole *Revelations* is a book of rejoicing in God) Julian considers praise as a gathering of momentum within. Then, as a river bursting its banks (my image), she sees it overflow into ecstatic words of delight: 'Good Lord, I thank you, blessed be your name.'

Julian expects her 'even-Christians' to know such times, and doubtless we have all experienced them. But she is too realistic to leave it there, and writing as always from experience, she continues: 'Sometimes when our hearts are dry or without feeling, or when we are assaulted by temptation, then we are driven by reason and grace to call upon our Lord, rehearsing his blessed passion and great goodness.' It is thus that the sacrifice of praise and thanksgiving finds its fulfilment, for left to our natural inclinations we would not be engaged in blessing God at such times.

Julian is beckoning us to allow the heart to be established in praise through repeated acts of blessing. The Eucharist and Daily Office, arrow prayers shot from the heart, repetitive prayers offered in the spirit of thankfulness such as the 'Our Father', the 'Gloria', the 'Hail Mary', together with those of our choice taken perhaps from the psalms, are all means whereby the heart may learn to beat in the joy and stillness of God.

The need of a short prayer

Praise is thus carried over into periods when we cannot consciously be engaged in it. There will be occasions each day when a new impulse needs to be given, not simply at the regular set times, but sometimes at odd moments, the halt at the traffic lights, the queue in the shop, the walk down the familiar street. Such periods will alternate with those in which the heart is simply to rest in the silence of God. In some such ways we are enabled to grow into becoming a focus of blessing which cannot but shed its portion of light on the world around.

For this to come about, however, we need some short prayer of our choice, always available to us. This is not in place of spontaneous acts of praise but supportive of them. It is used simply for the praise of God even when no specific cause of praise is present to the mind. It may be recited aloud, or silently, or simply in the mind over and over again, eventually becoming established in the heart. It is in that way that there will be formed the heart 'whose pulse will be, thy praise'.

'Praise him, praise him, Jesus is Lord' is one suggestion. Or, 'May Jesus Christ be praised'. St Peter says (1 Peter 3:15) 'Hold Christ in your hearts in reverence as Lord'. Each time we say from the heart either of these phrases we are doing just that. Or the single word 'Alleluia' (see p. 45), an ejaculation of praise with no precise meaning, rooted in the heart and resonating in the depths, may supply to some just what is needed.

Later, we shall examine more deeply the practice of repetitive praise and prayer and the reasoning which lies behind it. Suffice it to say now that prayer is a holding on to God until we move into the knowledge that we are being held. How God may be held in reverence in our hearts will be the subject we shall explore later.

The stirring of the will

Writing this page on what is sometimes called 'Stir-up Sunday' (Christmas puddings in the making were traditionally stirred on that day), I am reminded by the collect that it is our wills that are to be stirred and not our emotions.

'Stir up, we beseech thee, O Lord, the wills of thy faithful people . . .'[15] The reference is to 'the bringing forth of good works' but it is equally true in the realm of praise.

The will is to be stirred to praise when the heart is cold and the emotions flat or even contrary. Hence the *sacrifice* of praise of which the New Testament speaks.

For example, it is likely to be impossible to *feel* grateful to someone who criticises us harshly. The way forward is to behave with as good grace as we can, as if we are grateful both in the realm of praise and action.

The response depends on the will and not the emotions. It is simply to put into effect the command of Jesus that we are to love our enemies and do good to those who trouble us.

To act against the feelings is unfortunately labelled by some as hypocrisy. A little reflection will show that to carry that precept through to its logical conclusion would mean a complete breakdown of civilised behaviour.

Can we praise God for our past sins?

Let us take this teaching a little further. I suppose most of us have often thanked God for the forgiveness of our sins. What is written next makes sense only in the context of our forgiveness and the daily renewal of our life in Christ. Unless this is true, this page should be taken no further.

If it is true that we can and should praise God for everything, then we may and should praise God for allowing every sin we have ever committed.

Impossible, you may say, my sins were evil. But I am not saying that evil is praiseworthy, only that God allowing evil is praiseworthy.

Impossible again, you may reply, my sins have hurt others. That is true, yet we are all hurt people, we are all, every one, wounded spirits, and as soon as we can begin praising God for our hurts we are in the way of healing.

The same will be true of those whom my sins have damaged. Yet no one is wounded beyond repair, and God's healing salve is within the reach of all.

The grace of God is the one commodity left to humankind which is 'without money and without price' (Isaiah 55:1). If we do not believe that grace is within the grasp of every wounded soul we have no gospel to proclaim.

Not as wounds but as honours

When we look back on our lives and recall our sins we may gratefully reflect that these sins are in large measure responsible for bringing us to where we now are: committed members of the Church of Christ, struggling indeed, and often falling, yet ever looking afresh in hope to the one who will yet again rescue us and lead us on.

'And now, Lord, what is my hope: truly my hope is even in thee' (Psalm 39:8). Apart from falls which have brought me low it is likely my hope would still be in myself.

It remains true that our past sins have wounded, and it may be that the wounds have been deep and ugly, but in our Saviour Christ these wounds are being transfigured so that at the last they shall be seen by God 'not as wounds but as honours'.

These words are from Julian's *Revelations of Divine Love*.[16] Julian sees us all (with herself) as wounded souls, yet it has been shown to her that our wounds taken to God and transfigured in Christ shall one day be seen as our glory and not our shame.

The transfiguration of the good

> Christ transfigures everything in us, the good as well as the
> bad. In every person there is a wound. Moan about this
> wound and it becomes a torment. Transfigured by Christ it
> becomes a locus of energy, a source of creativity, giving rise
> to a potential for communion, fellowship and understanding.

The words above are from Père Schultz of Taizé. Note especially
that the good is to be transfigured as well as the bad. Too often,
we forget this.

For example, a person may be doing noble and conscientious
work in caring for the sick, visiting in the parish, raising money
for the needy, or preaching the gospel. Yet in so far as this
work is a fulfilling of emotional needs it awaits transfiguration
in Christ.

To be continually looking Godwards in the spirit of praise and
thanksgiving in whatever work we undertake is to enable this
transfiguration to take place.

A shining example in today's world of the transfiguration of the
good may be found in Mother Teresa of Calcutta. Condescension
and patronage, the telltale marks of our partially redeemed state,
are swallowed up in humility, and everything is laid at the feet
of God in praise and thanksgiving.

The blessing of acceptance

Praise involves acceptance. If you praise God for your children or your friends it means you have accepted them.

And if we can truly thank and praise God for allowing our past sins (it may take a lifetime and more of grace and endeavour) it means we have accepted ourselves, our blemishes, our oddities, and in that there is great enrichment; though, naturally, we continue to the end to lay our frailties before God that his cleansing love may work upon them.

I believe that when we can from the depths of the heart, in the power of the Holy Spirit, rejoicing in the saving work of Jesus, thus thank and praise God, we shall at that moment be truly humble and ready to enter into the fullness of God's joy. This may be a deeply consoling thought to some people. God truly wants us to learn to thank and praise him for everything.

Even so, this practice, whilst it brings with it great blessing, admits us into a dangerous area of the spiritual life. It needs, perhaps, to be said again that it makes no sense apart from the acceptance of our forgiveness, and our experience of daily renewal in Christ. It is a message for the faithful, for those whom Julian called her even-Christians ('men and women who, for God's love, hate sin and turn themselves to do God's will'), and not for those who are not seeking to bring their lives under the captivity of Christ.

Yet, as we shall see, even for the Christian there remains the danger of the good news of the gospel being perverted to selfish ends.

A danger answered

Paul gives expression to this danger when, after proclaiming God's free forgiveness in Christ, he imagines an objector saying that his message may encourage some to sin that God's grace may the more abound. Paul's response (Romans 6:1–3; 5) is swift and sharp.

> Shall we sin to our heart's content and see how far we can exploit the grace of God? What a ghastly thought! We who have died to sin, how could we live in sin a moment longer! Have you forgotten that all of us who were baptised into Jesus Christ were by that very action sharing in his death? ... If we have, as it were, shared his death, let us rise and live our new lives with him.

Julian, also fearful lest some might abuse her message of God's inexhaustible love, answers more gently:

> If because of all this spiritual comfort one were foolish enough to say: 'if this is true it is a good thing to sin because the reward will be greater', or to hold sin less sinful, then beware! Should such a thought come it would be untrue and would come from the enemy of this very love which tells of all this comfort. The same blessed love tells us that we should hate sin for love's sake alone. We are to hate sin absolutely. Our hatred of sin will be like God's hatred of sin, our love of the soul like God's.[17]

It is so and it is well

Let us then not be afraid to apply Paul's principle of praising God for everything to thanking him for permitting our sins. He has not allowed them beyond the extent to which he can turn them into good.

Though frozen hard as fact in history, our sins remain fluid in what they may yield as value in the present.

They serve to remind us of our frailty, of our constant need for God, and of the enduring nature of his love which will never desert us however grievously we fall.

In praising God for the past lies acceptance, and in acceptance lies healing, and in this context healing especially from guilt-ridden memories.

We may bring these thoughts to their end (and climax) by quoting Julian's memorable words from a closing chapter of her book:

> When judgement is given and we are all brought up above, then we shall see clearly the secrets now hidden from us. In that day not one of us will want to say, 'Lord, if it had been done this way, it would have been well done'. But we shall all say with one voice, 'Lord, blessed may you be, for it is so, and it is well. And now we see truly that all things were done as it was ordained before anything was made.'[18]

Uncertainty and praise

Paul's command to thank and praise God for everything can be extended to other areas of our lives. Suppose I am uncertain about something. Should I, for example, speak out or remain silent? Should I buy this car, this house, these clothes? Is my call to celibacy or to marriage? Uncertainty can cause great suffering and at times it feels as if it would pull us apart.

First, having put the matter into God's hands, we may try by all reasonable means to resolve the uncertainty. It may be the scales will balance, then a little later one is down, and then the other, and then balancing again. And so it goes on.

Now is the time to put reasoning aside, at least for the time being, and to start to praise God in and for our uncertainty. At the same time we lift up its pain as an offering to God.

Probably most of us crave after a well-marked way where we may feel secure. The prospect of leaving the road for uncharted country may fill us with foreboding and fear. Uncertainty may make our path so uncomfortable that we are almost driven into the arms of God, the only sure refuge when familiar landmarks have dropped away.

To praise God for allowing our uncertainty, understanding the good which may flow from it, not only makes it easier to bear but holds us open to receive its fruits. Chief of these will be the deepening of our relationship with God, and since our growth is dependent upon relationship that must be of great importance.

And what of the uncertainty itself? It may not be that in this practice it will be removed, though undoubtedly we are sometimes given an inward intuitive knowledge of what should be done.

Fear and depression and praise

How may our teaching be applied if we are fearful or depressed? Some fears and depressions are so disorientating to the personality that professional help should in the first place be sought. But I have in mind here especially those fears and sorrows which are our common lot, those in which the will, through grace, can still be summoned to the praise of God.

Acts of praise in the power of faith when the spirit is dulled and the heart is low have upon us a similar effect as the sun on mist at the start of a new spring day.

For a while it may seem that nothing is happening, but by midday the mist is gone and we can bask in the warmth which embraces us. So, too, in the continual blessing of God comes the dispersal of our fears, our restlessness, our gloom and heaviness of soul.

Yet there will be days when the haze remains. We have to be clear that the purpose of this book is missed if praise is seen as a formula for manipulating God to our own ends. The important thing is not the disappearance of the fear or depression. The important thing is that God is being praised. For, as we have seen, to praise God *is* to triumph.

Although praise is, as we are reminded at every Eucharist, 'our duty and our joy', we are not to expect those elements to be equally present in every act of praise. Usually there will be a blending of the two, but sometimes praise may be pure duty, at others pure joy.

Yet always through praise a relationship is being sustained and developed. Praise is positive. Its tendency is always to banish negativity. And negativity is the source of much depression and fear.

Sexuality and praise and thanksgiving

I recall a book by a Christian minister of my youth in which readers were invited to avert their eyes from pictures in art galleries which aroused their sexual feelings.

That advice may be correct at a certain stage but for the mature it will hardly do. Such do well to view the work of art in a spirit of praise for its merit and for the beauty of the human form.

Sexuality is one of God's most precious gifts and may be channelled into many creative forms. One of these is praise itself; and nothing is more creative than praise.

Celibates who fail to recognise their sexuality are likely to be lacking in vitality and may be permanently tired and jaded. Sexual energies cannot be re-directed into creative channels so long as they are repressed. They must be accepted and (within the call to celibacy) be allowed to become partners in Christian living.

Everyone, however, should know their capacities. It is as with rich food which is strengthening in moderation, whereas too much puts an intolerable strain on the system. Of course we may offer the sacrifice of fasting. And that principle applies to all areas of our life.

Human nature is a frail commodity and without discipline may land us in trouble. It is necessary to strike a balance. If we are too severe with our sexuality we are liable to freeze. If we are too lenient, the danger is we shall drown.

Praise and thanksgiving offer the best way forward. For those who live in the spirit of praise the intimacies of married life will necessarily be caught up in it. Paul, as so often, has the word. 'Everything created by God is good, and nothing is to be rejected if it is received with thanksgiving, for then it is consecrated by the word of God and prayer.' (1 Timothy 4:4, 5)

Bitterness and praise

Suppose you have feelings of bitterness towards another. Try praising God for the person who has drawn out your bitterness.

I put it that way because it is not the other person who has made you bitter. You must have been that way before he or she came along. What the other has done is to act as a catalyst, drawing out the bitterness which was already there.

Strange as it may seem you have been done a favour. You have been given the chance to know yourself, a chance which might otherwise have been missed. And you cannot deal with a self which you do not know.

To praise God in the presence of negative and destructive emotions such as bitterness, anger, jealousy and the like (and the praise of God is always positive: it is *God* who is being praised and not the emotions) means that you are accepting them for as long as God allows them to remain. And it means that you are recognising and owning to this little bit of truth about yourself.

You are opening out the dark side of yourself, exposing it to God that his healing light may rest upon it.

More on the dark side

If we are to follow C J Jung this dark or shadow side (which is so painful to acknowledge and hence is so often suppressed), is ninety percent gold, and must not be permanently banned from recognition if it is to yield up what is good within it to be integrated with the conscious life.

We should note that it needs to be acknowledged and recognised, but that it should not be acted out where to do so would transgress moral norms. This may well be a difficult tension to hold, and not everyone will be ready for it. That is why the individuation process, as Jung calls it, may often find its expression in middle or later life. Individuation has been described as the conscious realisation and integration of all the possibilities immanent in the individual.

If the shadow is permanently repressed, psychic energy is being dammed up which might otherwise be available to the conscious life. And psychic energy available to consciousness is being used up in holding it down. So we are losers on both counts. It is little wonder if we are listless and tired.

Julian of Norwich, in the *Revelations*, says in the language of her day very much what Jung says in today's medium.

> We can never attain to the full knowledge of God until we have first known our own soul thoroughly. Until our soul reaches its full development we can never be completely holy. In other words, not until our sensuality has been raised to the level of our essential being. . .[19] Our fragmented lives are [to be] knit together and made perfect man, and by giving and yielding ourselves through grace to the Holy Spirit we are made whole.[20]

Quotable quotes

I have come to believe that the prayer of praise is the highest form of communion with God and one that always releases a great deal of power into our lives.

Praising him is not something we do because we feel good but rather is an act of obedience . . . There is a ladder of praise and I believe that everyone without exception can begin to praise God right now in whatever situation they may find themselves.

For our praise to reach the perfection God wants for us, it needs to be free of any thoughts of reward. Praise is not another way of bargaining with the Lord.

Praising God with a pure heart means we must let God cleanse our hearts from impure motives and hidden designs. We have to experience the dying to self so that we can live again in Christ in newness of mind and spirit.

Praise is based on a total and joyful acceptance of the present as part of God's loving, perfect will for us. Praise is not based on what we think or hope will happen in the future.

It is, of course, a fact that when we honestly praise God, something *does* happen as a result. His power obviously flows into the situation, and we will notice, sooner or later, a change in us or around us. The change may be that we come to experience a real joy and happiness in the midst of what once appeared to be a miserable situation or the situation may change. But this is a *result* of praise, and must not be the motivation for praise.[21]

Praising God for those for whom we pray

We should praise God for those for whom we pray. Paul lays considerable stress upon this. Three times in his epistles Paul links supplication with thanksgiving. In addition, on eight occasions in as many epistles Paul tells his readers that he thanks God for them in his prayers.

Try telling a friend that you pray for her daily; and then tell another that you thank and praise God for her daily in your prayers. See what different reactions you get!

To thank God for those for whom we pray is a safeguard against condescension which always threatens the purity of intercessory prayer. Yet we have to admit that in our present state of spiritual poverty there are (as every news bulletin may remind us) those for whom it may be impossible to praise God with personal integrity.

Fortunate, then, are those familiar with the rosary. The first part of each 'Hail Mary' is an expression of praise to Jesus and Mary. The second part ('pray for us sinners . . .') cuts across any suggestion of patronage by placing ourselves at the same level of dependence and need as those for whom we pray.[22]

In praying for others they become indebted to us. In giving thanks for others in our prayers we become indebted to them. This is usually a healthier situation. An interchange is best of all:

> Won't you let me be your servant,
> Let me be as Christ to you.
> Pray that I may have the grace to
> Let you be my servant too.

Praise enlarges our hearts towards those for whom we pray. And their hearts towards us. And that is the beginning of the answer to our prayer.

A thorn in the flesh

Paul tells us (2 Corinthians 12:7) that there was given to him a 'thorn in the flesh, the messenger of Satan sent to buffet me'. We do not know what form this took but evidently it was painful and distressing.

The Bible is as wise in its silences as in what it reveals. Its silence as to the nature of Paul's complaint allows us to identify with him.

Paul did not begin by praising God for his affliction, but instead he asked God three times to remove it. The reply came: 'My grace is sufficient for you, for my strength is made perfect in weakness.'

It was then that Paul started praising: 'Most gladly will I glory in my infirmities, that the power of Christ may rest upon me.'

The spirit of praise and thanksgiving always releases power, whereas that of grumbling and discontent blocks the path of the Holy Spirit.

> He lays upon everyone he longs to bring into his bliss something that is no blame in his sight, but for which they are blamed and despised in this world – scorned, mocked and cast out. He does this to offset the harm they should otherwise have from the pomp and vainglory of this earthly life, and to make their road to him easier, and to bring them higher in his joy without end.[23]

Few people can have been more creative than Helen Keller – blind and deaf since birth – who said: 'I thank God for my handicaps, for through them I have found myself, my work and my God.'

Praising God in a suffering world

What are we to make of the teaching here given in the light of concentration camps, ethnic cleansing and besieged cities? May God still be praised?

I would find it impossible from the security of my English home to exhort my several Bosnian Christian friends to praise God as their country violently crumbles before their eyes. I imagine every reader would feel the same. Even so it needs to be said that it is the clear teaching of the New Testament that just as forgiveness cannot be limited to 'seven times', so too there are no limits to the situations in which God is to be praised.

Thus Peter writes to the Church, 'Rejoice (which is to say thank and praise God) that you participate in the sufferings of Christ' (1 Peter 4:13), and we know well enough what those sufferings were. And Jesus says to his followers that they are to thank and praise God when they are persecuted for his sake (Matthew 5:11–12). Nor do these exhortations stand alone.

Paul, who bids us to rejoice with those who rejoice, adds that we are to weep with those who weep (Romans 12:15). Yet in sharing the sorrows of the suffering we are not to be as those without hope: 'rejoicing in hope', writes Paul in the same passage. Thereby every situation is in some measure redeemed.

What was a bad Friday in Jerusalem has become Good Friday for the Church. These words should not be dismissed as glib or empty. For in Calvary is set the pattern to which every life in Christ must conform: 'Except a grain of wheat fall into the ground and die . . .' (John 12:24)

Our present life is an unfinished symphony and the final movements are yet to be revealed. Rather than speculate on the purpose of the trials which afflict others, we would do better to consider whether we ourselves withold our compassion and do not do what we can to alleviate their suffering.

Our truest benefactors

What is there we can do to help in the horrific situations which confront us today? There are practical ways open to almost all of us. For some that will mean the application of political or economic, social or medical skills. For the great majority it will mean the sacrifice of money or goods.

Practical relief, and the money which feeds it, may never be neglected. Even so, it is, I believe, only prayer which can reach the root causes which lie behind our cosmic sickness.

In particular, faithfulness in offering the sacrifice of praise at the level given us has, I believe, an effect far beyond our own special concerns or the concerns of those immediately around us. But it has to be added that here we are in an area where argument is useless and faith alone can be our guide.

I can only state that I believe contemplatives – and to every true contemplative belongs the spirit of thankfulness and praise – are our greatest benefactors whether or not they have anything discernible to offer in the way of material benefits.

In particular, though by no means only, it is the religious communities which are the lifeblood of the Church. If we could but share with them in the measure appropriate to our state, their continual sacrifice of praise and thanksgiving (continual because the temper of mind and spirit generated by worship will govern the activities and relationships of daily life), the priorities and values of the nations would be transformed. And who can say what might not then follow?

Praise makes good practical sense

To praise God in every situation is, as we have seen, the surest means of remaining creatively open to the possibilities which may flow from it. And this is true both for situations which directly affect us and those in which others are caught up.

Even from our limited perspective we may often be aware of the potential for good arising from circumstances which appear disastrous to the one involved. The loss of money and possessions, an illness involving an enforced rest from a busy life, a prison sentence, a bereavement, may come as a shattering blow to the one who experiences them, yet to wiser friends it may not be difficult to understand how God has suffered them to be that they may be turned to good account.

In praising God in and for such events, secretly, one may add, and not in the presence of the one experiencing them (at least not until he or she can join in the thanksgiving) the situation is effectively placed trustfully in God's hands. Moreover, acceptance is assured, and a judgemental attitude is averted.

When disaster strikes, the one who sympathises simply by bemoaning the victim's bad luck, will be a less true friend than the other who, when the time is ripe, can point to the constructive opportunities which the situation offers. Those who live in the spirit of praise are likely to be best equipped for that.

The challenge of praise

To write these exhortations is much easier than to put them into practice. To praise God in contrary circumstances is not congenial to human nature, and means repeatedly cutting across our natural inclinations. It calls in full measure for courage, faith and perseverance.

It is a goal we may set ourselves, but it is only by relying on God's grace at every turn that it can be achieved. We are not to be discouraged by failures. Falling and getting up, confession and restoration, sorrow and joy, death and resurrection: this is the underlying pattern of Christian discipleship.

It has been encouragingly said that our choice as Christians is not between success and failure, but rather between being a glorious failure like Peter who, after every fall, accepted the humiliation and returned to his Lord, or a miserable failure whereby we become a prey to hopelessness and despair.[24]

Paul speaks of the Christian life as an interior crucifixion, a slow putting to death of the contrary elements within us, and he is well aware of the difficulty and suffering involved.

Not that suffering is the final note. Those who die with Christ shall one day reign with him (2 Timothy 2:12) and share the joy of his resurrection.

More on the will and emotions

Praise cannot always have about it the spontaneity manifested in times of emotional fervour as was experienced in the early days of the Church.

Of the first converts, made in response to Peter's pentecostal speech, we read that they met 'day after day in the Temple, taking their meals in one another's houses, eating with glad and humble hearts, praising God and enjoying the good-will of all'. (Acts 2:46ff)

Such euphoria must inevitably wear thin as the pressures and responsibilities of everyday life begin once again to make themselves felt.

Praise has to be worked at if it is to be sustained. But in so doing we do well to recall that it belongs in the first place to the will, and only secondarily (by which is not meant unimportantly) to the emotions (see p. 19).

Thus it is that Paul repeatedly tells us to rejoice. It is interesting to note that he never tells us to be joyful, though certain translations make him say just that. Rejoicing belongs to the will: being joyful to the emotions. We cannot command the emotions. But through grace we can give expression and direction to the will.

In the long run the emotions will follow the bent of the will, and joy and praise and thankfulness will flood our lives.

But this has to be waited for. The times and seasons are in God's hands and not in ours.

Paul more realistic than some translators

As an example of what has been said we may take Paul's letter to the Philippians. Here he writes (Philippians 4:4) 'Rejoice in the Lord always, and again I say rejoice'. So runs the *Authorised Version*, and the American *Revised Standard Version* (remaining true to the Greek) follows that translation.

Compare with the rendering of the same passage in the *Jerusalem Bible*: 'I want you to be happy, always happy in the Lord; I repeat, what I want is your happiness.'

Recognising, perhaps, the weakness of this translation the *New Jerusalem Bible* offers: 'Always be joyful in the Lord, I repeat be joyful.' But it still misses the precision of St Paul's words as, too, does the *New English Bible* which gives, 'I wish you joy in the Lord always; again I say all joy be yours'.

Paul is too realistic to say any of these things. What he says is, 'Rejoice, rejoice in the Lord at all times, and again I tell you to rejoice'.

Paul reinforces his theme in two of his letters (Ephesians 5:19ff and Colossians 3:16ff) where he exhorts his readers to be active in thanking and praising God in psalms and hymns.

In effect Paul's message is: 'Even when your heart is dull, your mind sluggish, your emotions contrary (as well as when your heart is full) in such measure as may be given you, offer to God the praise and thanksgiving which is his due.'

This is not the same thing as bidding us to be happy or joyful though, ultimately, as we respond to Paul's exhortation, the joy of which modern translations speak will be ours.

The discipline of praise

Every mature Christian understands the importance of this teaching of Paul. No priest, no monk or nun, no oblate of a community would be advised to say their office only on days when they felt so inclined.

The office – and of course the Eucharist – is the Church's daily offering of praise and thanksgiving, and we are to associate ourselves with this offering, not according to mood or emotion, but as part of a settled discipline, forming in us the habit of prayer and praise.

The Book of Common Prayer speaks of praise and thanksgiving as 'our bounden duty'; *The Alternative Service Book*, as we have already noted, calls it 'our duty and our joy'. Both books call us to exercise it 'at all times and in all places'. It follows that praise, whatever else it may be, is an act of obedience. If that thought be absorbed we shall be greatly encouraged when passing through the dry patches which belong to every Christian life.

'Who going through the vale of misery use it for a well; and the pools are filled with water' (Psalm 84:6). Even the seemingly barren ground becomes fertile if watered with praise.

The prayer life built in response to the feelings of the moment is as a house built on sand; it is powerless against the wind and the storm. That which is built on the fortress of the will – not despising the emotions, for their right functioning is essential to a full Christian life, yet seeing them as subordinate to the will – that is the house which can withstand times of testing when they come.

Leading to mantric praise

In spite of what has been written it is important to realise that we do not have to praise God for any particular gifts or benefits he has bestowed on us. We are to learn to praise him quite simply for what he is.

We may praise God for great works of art or music, for the beauty of nature, for the blessings of health or sleep or food, for his loving Providence, for his acts of redemption and restoration through the cross and resurrection of Jesus, and it is good that we should do so. But we may be taken beyond all this to the purest form of praise, the praise of God for himself alone. As Psalm 146 puts it:

> Praise the Lord. Praise the Lord, O my soul: while I live I will praise the Lord: while I have any being I will sing praises to my God.

If we are to live at this deeper level of praise, a praise which is offered without any specific event to evoke it, a praise which does not depend on our calling to our imagination some object of praise, and, furthermore, a praise to be exercised 'at all times and in all places', we shall need a short prayer to which we can turn again and again, a prayer which will eventually become rooted in the heart. We shall refer to this as a praise mantra.

We touched on this in our reading on page 18 and we suggested several praise forms. In taking this thought forward we are led to consider mantric prayer; or in this context mantric praise. Either way, the underlying principle is the same. We simply take the prayer/praise mantra of our choice, and by repeated use allow it to become established in the heart.

Repetitive or mantric prayer

The word 'mantra' is suspect to some Christians because they associate it exclusively with non-Christian faiths. But it is the concept and not the word which matters. Many like to have what they call an 'anchor phrase' to which they can repeatedly turn, and that is precisely what a mantra is. It is this which may help the divine presence to be held perpetually in the heart, something which St Peter, as we have seen, urges his readers to do.

As the form of words is repeated again and again (silently or aloud) the mind is drawn into them (mindless gabbling is no part of mantric prayer), and eventually they become established in the heart. The prayer then continues at this level.

Mantric prayer is feared by some because they think it contradicts the words of Jesus: 'Use not vain repetitions as the heathen do, for they think they shall be heard for their much speaking.' (Matthew 6:7)

But the operative word is 'vain'. An operation is vain if it does not fulfil the purpose for which it was intended. Thus if I try to hammer a nail into a piece of wood and it does not penetrate the surface the work is vain. But if it penetrates even a hundredth of an inch with each blow, then the operation is useful and not vain.

Repetition runs right through life. Consider the rotating wheels of a car, the repeated steps when walking, stitch after stitch in knitting. These are not vain because each rotation, each step, each stitch, is made from a different starting point than the one before.

So it is with mantric prayer. So long as the intention or desire to pray, and to be conformed to God's will, is present, each prayer is uttered from a new starting point, each successive point being closer to the heart of God.

'Put your mind into your heart, and stand in the presence of God all the day long' says an ancient teacher on prayer. It is the mantra which helps us to do this.

A continual deepening of spiritual quality

The following passage will serve to reinforce the argument of the last page. It should help us to understand that we have nothing to fear, but much to gain, from repetitive or mantric prayer, where the desire for God remains constant.

We are not to think that long continuance of the same cry to God means no change. The outward expression may be the same, but the force of any two acts can never be the same.

The fact that five seconds ago I said 'Jesus, I love you', wrought a change in me, so that when I say the same words again, I bring to them a stronger spirit of love and devotion to our Lord than would have been possible in the first instance.

The first act brought me into a closer and fuller union with him, and although I may not perceive it, so profound a change was wrought in me that each succeeding act makes upon my character an increasingly powerful impress, the force and effect of which is ever mounting.

So, strictly speaking there is no repetition. It is not the same but a different work that is done.

Thus, as we go on in the work of prayer, the soul does not, cannot, abide in any one stay. There is a continual deepening of spiritual quality, and an intensification of love, and with love all the other virtues flower every moment into newer and richer things.[25]

Choosing a praise mantra

The words on the previous page, 'Jesus, I love you', would make a good prayer mantra. But it is with a praise mantra we are now concerned. Bear with me if I put down simply my own practice and allow the reader to adapt their own way from there.

I take a rosary, and on the medallion (which is the point where the circlet of the rosary joins the pendant) I say an 'Our Father'. Still on the medallion I say three times, 'Save and help us that we may praise you'.

Next come the ten beads of the first decade. On each of these is said, 'Praise him, praise him, Jesus is Lord. May Jesus Christ be praised'. If the rosary is being said with another then one of us says the first half of the prayer and the other the second.

The decade is concluded by saying a 'Gloria' ('Glory be . . .') on the spaced bead following the decade. On the same bead, 'Save and help us that we may praise you' is again said three times. The praise mantra follows on each decade bead, then a 'Gloria' on the spaced bead, and so on until the circlet is completed.

The exercise, which can be repeated as often as one likes, keeps the spirit of praise alive in the heart, and enables the heart to continue in praise when the words have dropped away.

As we go round we may either let our minds be drawn into the words being said (in this case just praising Jesus because he is Lord) or the praise may be offered for some person or cause (see p. 16), which can be changed as desired.

The rosary is often shunned by non-Catholics because of its association with Marian devotion which may not be in their tradition. This is a mistake. The instrument of the rosary should be seen as a piano which will take an infinite variety of tunes. The psalter offers an almost inexhaustible supply. The rule is to find a form with which we feel comfortable and then to stay with it. Even so, another form may suit another occasion.

A classic description of mantric prayer

The following passage from the Sufi mystic Al-Ghazali is a classic description of mantric prayer.

> Let [the worshipper] see that nothing save God most High enters his heart. Then, as he sits in solitude, let him not cease from saying continuously with his tongue, 'Allah, Allah' keeping his thought on it.
>
> At last he will reach a state when the motion of his tongue will cease, and it will seem as though the word flowed from it.
>
> Let him persevere in this until all trace of motion is removed from his tongue, and he finds his heart persevering in the thought. Let him persevere until the form of words, its letters and shape, is removed from his heart and there remains the idea alone, as though clinging to his heart, inseparable from it.
>
> So far, all is dependent on his will and choice. But to bring the mercy of God does not stand in his will or choice.
>
> He has now laid himself bare to the breathings of that mercy, and nothing remains but to wait what God will open to him, as God has done after this manner to prophets and saints.
>
> If he follows the above course he may be sure that the light of the Real will shine out in his heart.[26]

The above principle applies whether we use a short form such as 'Abba', 'Jesus', or 'Alleluia', or longer forms such as are to be found in this book.

Using a mantra

Note especially from the quotation on the previous page that we cannot command the mercy of God. The most we can do is through grace to dispose ourselves to receive it. We have to wait for it as the parched earth waits for the rain to fall.

Using a mantra is rather like pedalling a bicycle. On the bad days when the wind is against us we have to pedal all the time. Then there are calm days when the road is flat, and after pedalling for a while we can allow our momentum to carry us along. And there are yet other days when we are on a downward slope and can free-wheel all the way.

So the mantra comes and goes. We cannot tell beforehand how the Holy Spirit will direct our prayers. Often it will be that what seems suitable today is different tomorrow.

In saying the mantra it is well to remember that it is what happens at the level of the heart which is ultimately important. The words of prayer act as the banks of a river keeping it deep and flowing. But although the banks are necessary it is the river which really matters.

And the river stands for the inclination of the heart towards God. Is the heart at praise? It may not always seem that way but it will become so if we have the courage and faith to persevere.

We may take the river imagery a little further and note that as it flows into the ocean the banks drop away. So the words cease, and we are left in the silence of the heart before God.[27]

A fable from the East

The following fable gives a further insight into mantric prayer:

On a desert island several miles from the mainland there stood a temple with a thousand silver bells. In stormy weather the bells would ring, and it was said that anyone on the mainland who could hear them would immediately become enlightened. In the course of time the island sank into the sea. Yet it was said that from beneath the waters the temple bells still rang out, and that enlightenment awaited anyone who could hear them.

A young man anxious for enlightenment travelled to the shore nearest to the sunken island. There he sat under a palm tree day after day straining to hear the temple bells. It was of no avail. All he could hear was the roar of the waves pounding the sea-shore, and this irritated him because it seemed they spoilt his chance of hearing the bells.

After many months he considered his task hopeless and decided to return home. He went back to his lodgings and packed his belongings. But before he left he went down once more to the sea-shore, this time to say goodbye to the tree and the sky and the sea. As he sat he found himself listening to the waves, and the sound became soothing and relaxing. And so he continued listening as they broke repeatedly upon the shore. All of a sudden and quite unexpectedly he heard the tinkle of a bell. And then another, and another, until they all rang out and he became enlightened.[28]

The silence beyond the mantra

Let us draw out the meaning of the fable. The enlightenment being sought was the true silence of the heart before God. It is this which lies beyond the mantra but it will not be found by attempting to listen for it directly. In the fable the temple bells were only heard when the seeker found himself listening to the waves. So (in our application of the fable) the silence will be found only when we listen to the mantra, only as we allow our awareness to be drawn into it as we say it over and over again.

Clergy and others who say offices will have observed the same principle at work as they allow their awareness to be drawn gently into the psalms and prayers and readings.

'How long shall I be in the world of voice?' cries John the solitary. 'In the invisible world there is no voice for not even voice can utter its mystery . . . When shall I be raised up to silence . . . to something which neither voice nor word can bring?'[29]

Yet word and voice can lead us, through the mantra, to the threshold where the silence of the heart begins. Always beyond the praise of which we have been speaking is the silent praise of the heart. It is this we have to be taken to if we are to experience the words quoted from George Herbert, 'a heart whose pulse may be, Thy praise'.

It was said of the late John Main, one of the great teachers of prayer of our generation, that his teaching could almost be reduced to three words: 'Say your mantra.' The mantra he taught was 'maranatha', an Aramaic phrase from the New Testament meaning 'Come, Lord, come'. To some readers that may appeal more than the mantra of praise presented here. But the rule is the same: 'Say your mantra.' So shall we be led to the contemplative heart of praise when the mantra has dropped away.

A delicacy of balance

Apart from its intrinsic worth, a praise mantra prepares the heart for spontaneous acts of praise and thanksgiving. It keeps the heart and mind alert for opportunities which might otherwise be missed. The two levels of praise, as we might call them, support and sustain one another.

The praise which proceeds from the heart is serene and peaceful. It is not 'noisy' or disturbing to others. The note of triumphalism is absent. When spoken or sung its volume is an unreliable indication of worth. 'Songs of Praise' may indeed be songs of praise but they do not become so simply by the raising of the decibel count.

True praise does not belong to the vocal cords but to the inmost self. Unless the heart is in some measure engaged, the utterance of the words whether in speech or song is worthless.

However, if there be, no matter how small, the desire to pray from the heart, speech and song may be an indispensable aid in fanning the inward spark into a flame. The utterance of words can be as a pair of bellows to the heart. Yet we need to work carefully. Bellows, if used too vigorously, may have the undesired effect of putting the fire out.

There is a delicacy of balance here. If you try too hard in vocal prayer your own ego can get in the way and produce just the opposite effect to that intended. And if you try too little, insufficient 'oxygen' will be reaching the embers of your heart.

We need to work steadily but gently. The heart needs to be coaxed rather than forced.

Praise must be quickened by love

Praise, as must be abundantly evident, is often demanding, and it can be no surprise that the New Testament speaks of the sacrifice of praise. 'Through Jesus, therefore, let us continually offer to God a sacrifice of praise – the fruit of lips that confess his name' (Hebrews 13:15). And, significantly, the writer adds (for the reality of praise is tested by the quality of life): 'Do not forget to do good and to share with others, for with such sacrifices God is pleased.' Sacrifice is costly, demanding perhaps the utmost we can bring.

Bare sacrifice, uninformed by love is of no worth. 'I may give all I possess to the needy, I may give my body to be burnt, but if I have no love I gain nothing by it.' (1 Corinthians 13:3)

Where sacrifice is quickened by love its burden is eased. Could we but experience sacrifice where love reigned supreme it would seem light and easy.

When praise is excited by love, however small and inadequate it may appear, that same love is deepened within. And thus it is that where praise is the expression of love, love is the fruit of praise.

Work at praise we must if its fruits are to be made evident in our lives. Sacrifice, informed by love, is the stuff of which life is made. We are not to be discouraged by our seeming lack of love. God asks nothing of us beyond our means. He accepts us where we are and looks only for such love and devotion as we are able to bring.

As but one example. If we praise God for those we are about to meet we shall quickly discover that we love them more. And they us!

The sacrifice of time

Praise demands the sacrifice of time. If we were not fallen creatures, the praise of God would come as naturally to us as the eating of our meals. But we must take ourselves as we are. It will be necessary to set aside each day times when we give ourselves over to the praise mantra of our choice. For we shall never learn to praise God everywhere all the time until we have first learnt to praise him somewhere some of the time.[30]

By praising God all the time we do not of course mean that the mind should always be consciously exercised in praise. It is rather that what is experienced at the conscious level during the set times continues at a subliminal level as we go about our daily tasks. This is true of all prayer and it is what we mean by 'recollection'.

Yet it must be that the spirit of praise will wear thin during the occupations of the day, and we may then once again set aside a time for the mantra. Or we may simply take advantage of odd moments, such as waiting for the kettle to boil, or the bus to arrive. Every day provides many opportunities.

It is a good thing to explore beyond the mantra and find forms of praise which make special appeal. We shall have a variety of needs according to our temperament and background. The 'Te Deum' in the Prayer Book is a classic expression of praise, and is a link with the worship of the Church through the centuries. We may note that praise here leads on to the acknowledgement of God's mercy. Since praise is self-emptying – the most self-emptying occupation open to us – it must help to ground the soul in humility. One might call that the test of the authenticity of praise.

The song of all creation

The Book of Common Prayer may also come to our aid in providing a pattern for mantric prayer. There is one mantra already latent in the subconscious of millions brought up in its use: 'Praise him, and magnify him for ever.' These words are offered for repetition thirty-two times in the Prayer Book praise of all creation known as the Benedicite. If this form be chosen then it may be best to use the canticle regularly. This will serve to activate the mantra, and at the same time to associate it with the rich imagery of the poem.

Words introduced earlier combine well with this praise form. 'Save and help us that we may praise you: praise him, and magnify him for ever.' If used with a companion, perhaps on the rosary, each partner takes one half of the verse.

We must not be alarmed in mantric praise or prayer when, after a while, we lose the awareness of the sense of the words we are reciting. This is a good sign provided the will is collected into what we are doing, and it means that the prayer is moving to the heart level rather than remaining at that of the mind. The deeper we go into mantric prayer (and yet more into prayer beyond the mantra) the more we shall encounter the emerging, unfolding and deeper self, and it is in this engagement that new energies of the spirit are released.

The paradox of the mantra is that it does most for us when it appears to be doing least. And what is done for us can never be separated from what is done for those around us – and beyond. The prayer or praise of the heart is a centre of energy – the creative energy of love – which moves into areas of which we can seldom be consciously aware. An old-time writer affirms that all humankind, living and departed, is helped in its practice (I hope he would allow 'all creation') and adds for good measure, 'you yourself are made clean and virtuous by it, as by no other'.[30]

Epilogue

In conclusion let me draw together the praise forms already suggested and offer one or two more.

'Praise him, praise him, Jesus is Lord: may Jesus Christ be praised.' This form combines well with the cover of this book which (with the title and author's name covered) makes an admirable icon of praise. The letters IHS at the centre of the picture are the first three Greek capitals for the name *Jesus*. As we look, we can, if it helps, recite the praise form. But, of course, we can use the picture or the mantra independently of one another.[31]

Adapting slightly from page 52 we have: 'Save and help us that we may praise you: praise him and glorify him for ever.'

As we have seen (p.32) those who use the traditional rosary need look no further for a praise and prayer mantra.

From the psalms we might take: 'O let my mouth be filled with your praise: that I may sing of your glory and honour all the day long.'[32] My experience is that this makes an excellent rosary praise with a *Gloria* on the spaced beads.

But what are we to do in times of temptation, darkness, fear when everything seems to be acting against us? We need a powerful cry at such times. I know of none better than this from the *ASB* canticle *Saviour of the world*: 'Make yourself known as our saviour and mighty deliverer: save and help us that we may praise you.'

> Lord, I will mean and speak thy praise,
>   Thy praise alone.
> My busie heart shall spin it all my dayes.
> And when it stops for want of store,
> Then will I wring it with a sigh or groan,
> That thou mayest have yet more.[33]

Notes

1 The priest referred to is Fr Christopher Bryant SSJE. The final sentence in an obituary written after his death in 1985 reads: 'He would listen and share the pain; then, leaning slightly forward with a gentle smile would enquire: Have you tried *thanking* God for it?'

2 From George Herbert's hymn *Teach me, my God and King*.

3 This extract is taken from chapter 15 of *A Serious Call to a Devout and Holy Life* by William Law.

4 John Koenig, *Rediscovering the New Testament* (HarperSanFrancisco, 1992).

5 See Julian of Norwich, *Revelations of Divine Love* (henceforth referred to as *RDL*), chapter 35.

6 *Look to the Glory: The Collected Sayings of Fr R M Benson SSJE*. (Society of St John the Evangelist, Bracebridge, Toronto, 1966).

7 G D Smith, *The Teaching of the Catholic Church* (Burns and Oates, 1948), p. 45.

8 *RDL*, chapter 11.

9 I owe the imagery here to R S Thomas who wrote of well-meaning intercessors: 'Does God listen to them, crouched as he is over the interminable problem of how not to cheat when the hell-born spirit appears to be winning?'

10 I have not seen George (Patterson/Pattison?) for 60 years. If anyone knows he is living please do put us in touch. He would be in his late eighties.

11 The first and last lines of George Herbert's poem, *Gratefulness*.

12 The Church of England's *Alternative Service Book* (ASB) of 1980. This is taken from the canticle, *Saviour of the world*, p. 57.

13 The blessing was written by the Very Revd Hugh Dickinson, Dean of Salisbury Cathedral, and is gratefully used here with his permission.

14 *RDL*, chapter 40.

15 *The Book of Common Prayer* (BCP). Collect of the 25th Sunday after Trinity.

16 *RDL*, chapter 39.

17 *RDL*, chapter 29.

18 *RDL*, chapter 85.

19 *RDL*, chapter 56.

20 *RDL*, chapter 58.

21 The quotations are taken from Merlin Carothers, *Prison to Praise* (Hodder & Stoughton, 1972), and, by the same author, *Power in Praise* (Kingsway Publications, 1986). I am gratefully indebted to both these books.

22 The full prayer runs: 'Hail Mary, full of grace, the Lord is with thee; blessed art thou among women and blessed is the fruit of thy womb, Jesus. Holy Mary, mother of God, pray for us sinners, now, and at the hour of our death.'

23 *RDL*, chapter 28.

24 I owe this thought to Maria Boulding's *The Celebration of Praise*.

25 Shirley Hughson OHC, *Contemplative Prayer* (Holy Cross Press, USA, 1955).

26 Taken from *The Encyclopedia of Mysticism*. The entry adds the following information about the Sufis: 'The great evangelical missionary to India of the last century, Henry Martyn, found the Sufis to be kindred spirits and

spoke of them as the "Methodists of the East". Though his teaching was uncompromisingly Christian they recognised him as one of them.'

Those new to the mantra may like to know of *The Way of a Pilgrim* which is a classic introduction through the *Jesus Prayer* of the Orthodox Church. There are several translations from the Russian available from good bookshops.

27 I have drawn here (and occasionally elsewhere) on my book *A Doorway to Silence: The Contemplative Use of the Rosary* (Darton, Longman & Todd, 1991).

28 My knowledge of the fable comes from the late Anthony de Mello. I have retold it more briefly.

29 Quoted from a lecture given by Maggie Ross.

30 I have adapted a parallel saying on prayer from the late Fr Jock Dalrymple.

31 The reader unfamiliar with icons may care to refer to chapter 13 of my book *With Pity Not With Blame* (Darton, Longman & Todd, 1981, reprinted 1993) where their meditative and contemplative use is described.

32 Psalm 71:7.

33 From one of several poems by George Herbert entitled *Praise*.

Addendum to notes 5, 8, 14, 16, 17, 18, 19, 20, 23.

Although this is not a book on Mother Julian of Norwich, reference has been made to her in many places, and the reader may be glad to have an additional note on her and her writings.

Julian was born in 1342. She was possibly educated by the nuns at Carrow, a Benedictine Priory on the outskirts of Norwich. She probably died in about 1420. Her burial place is unknown.

In the early hours of 8 May 1373, Julian received fifteen visions centred on the person and Passion of Jesus, and a sixteenth on the following night. She wrote them down with her meditations upon them in her book *The Revelations of Divine Love* which was completed in 1393. The work is known as a spiritual classic throughout the Christian world. It is the first book known to have been written by a woman in English.

At an unknown date after her visions Julian became an anchoress, a woman dedicated to the religious life, living permanently alone in her cell attached to St Julian's Church in Norwich. Following the custom of her time she would almost certainly have taken her name from the Church, which would then have been about four hundred years old.

Julian is remembered for the depth of her theological and devotional writing in which she sees God as all-compassionate love. She would remind us that there is no power in heaven or on earth which can prevent God from loving us. Even when we fall from grace God's love is not turned away but is following us, eager to take us back to himself so soon as we turn again. 'He is quick to clasp us to himself for we are his joy and his delight, and he is our salvation and our life.' At all times we are enfolded in God's love. 'In his love he wraps and holds us; he enfolds us for love and will never let us go.'

Two small books, *Enfolded in Love* and *In Love Enclosed* (both DLT) will introduce the non-specialist reader to Julian's spirituality and theology. Later, many will want to read her complete book of which there are several renderings in modern English.

To Joyce and David.

Our Duty and Our Joy

**Donated
in memory of Joy
through
the Friends of Julian of Norwich**

*It was good to have
news of you and you
both remain much in
my love and prayer*

*Pamela
rscj.*

11 Nov. 1995.

For
Geoffrey and Denise
Richard and Rosalind
and Edna
companions in prayer
who encouraged me